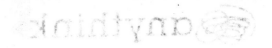

YOU'RE ANGRY

THROW A FIT
OR
TALK IT OUT?

You Choose the Ending

by Connie Colwell Miller • illustrated by Victoria Assanelli

Do you ever wish you could change a story or choose a different ending?

IN THESE BOOKS, YOU CAN!

Read along and when you see this:

WHAT HAPPENS NEXT?

Skip to the page for that choice, and see what happens.

In this story, Kendra does not want to go to bed. Will she throw a fit or will she talk about it? YOU make the choices!

It's a summer evening, and Kendra is playing hide-and-seek with her friends. It is finally her turn to seek. Kendra's dad calls, "Kendra! Time for bed!" But Kendra wants to keep playing.

WHAT HAPPENS NEXT?

→ If Kendra stomps her feet, turn the page.
If Kendra talks with her dad, turn to page 20. ←

Kendra is angry. She stomps her feet. "I don't want to go to bed!" she yells. "Kendra," her father repeats, "come inside now please."

WHAT HAPPENS NEXT?

If Kendra whines and cries, turn the page.
If Kendra goes to the door, turn to page 16.

"No! I want to play hide-and-seek!" Kendra whines. She begins to cry. Her father is upset. He says, "Kendra, I've asked you twice. Now *please* come inside."

WHAT HAPPENS NEXT?

→ If Kendra throws a fit, turn the page.

If Kendra goes inside, turn to page 14. ←

7

Kendra sees her father walking toward her. She knows he is going to take her inside. "I don't want to go to bed!" she shouts over and over again. She kicks her father.

TURN THE PAGE →

"Kendra, stop throwing a fit!" her father says. "You are going to bed whether you like it or not." He picks Kendra up and carries her to the house.

TURN THE PAGE →

"You can have this fit in your bed," Dad says. "And tomorrow, you may not play with your friends at all—you are grounded."

Kendra cries for awhile. Then she starts to calm down. "If I hadn't had a fit, I could still play with my friends tomorrow," Kendra realizes.

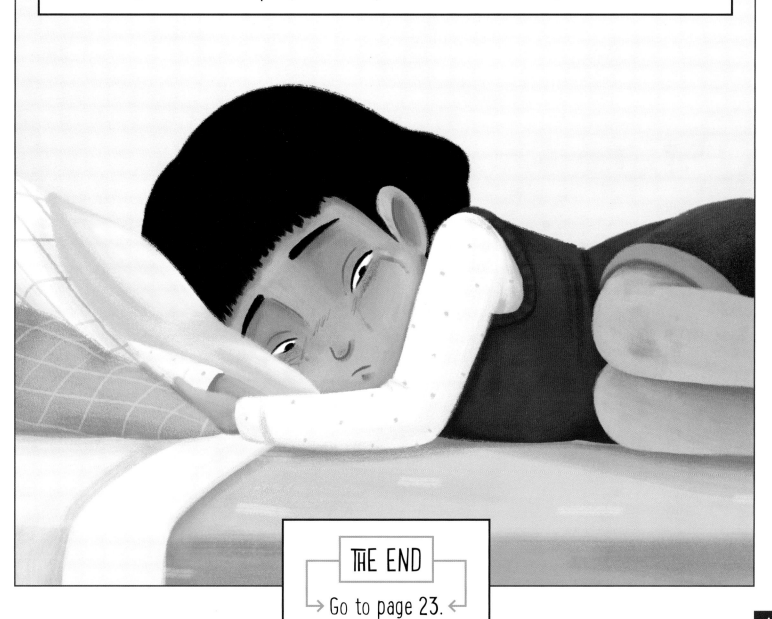

THE END

→ Go to page 23. ←

Kendra stomps inside. "Kendra, I don't like the way you are acting," Dad says. "I wish you had used words to tell me how you felt. No bedtime story tonight."

Kendra goes to bed. If she had talked to her dad about how she felt, maybe she could still play with her friends or have a bedtime story.

THE END

→ Go to page 23. ←

Kendra stomps to the house. Dad frowns and says, "Stomping your feet is not a good way to tell me how you feel. What could you do instead?"

TURN THE PAGE →

Kendra thinks. "I could talk to you," she says.
"I'm mad. I want to play with my friends."
Dad says, "I know. You can play tomorrow.
If you come in now, we can read a story."

Kendra goes in. She feels better after talking it out. She can read with her dad tonight and play again tomorrow.

THE END

⤷ Go to page 23. ⬸

Kendra feels angry. But she talks it out. "Dad," she says, "I really wanted to have my turn as seeker." Her dad smiles. "Okay," he says, "find your friends. Then come inside."

TURN THE PAGE $\rightarrow$

Because Kendra and her dad talked it out, she and her friends get to finish their game of hide-and-seek.

THE END

THINK AGAIN

- Which choices did you make for Kendra? How did that story end?
- Go back to page 3. Read the story again and pick different choices. How did the story change?
- Have you ever been so angry you threw a fit? What happened?

We are all free to make choices, but choices have consequences. What would YOU do if you were very angry?

For Kendra, who is just like one of our own.—C.C.M.

AMICUS ILLUSTRATED and AMICUS INK
are published by Amicus
P.O. Box 1329, Mankato, MN 56002
www.amicuspublishing.us

Library of Congress Cataloging-in-Publication Data
Names: Miller, Connie Colwell, 1976- author. | Assanelli, Victoria, 1984- illustrator.
Title: You're angry : throw a fit or talk it out? / by Connie Colwell Miller ;
    illustrated by Victoria Assanelli.
Description: Mankato, Minnesota : Amicus, [2018] | Series: Making good choices
Identifiers: LCCN 2016057212 (print) | LCCN 2017009558 (ebook) |
    ISBN 9781681511641 (library binding) | ISBN 9781681512549 (ebook) |
    ISBN 9781681522333 (pbk.)
Subjects: LCSH: Anger in children—Juvenile literature. | Decision making in
    children—Juvenile literature.
Classification: LCC BF723.A4 M554 2018 (print) | LCC BF723.A4 (ebook) |
    DDC 155.4/1247—dc23
LC record available at https://lccn.loc.gov/2016057212

Editor: Rebecca Glaser
Designer: Kathleen Petelinsek

Printed in North Mankato, Minnesota
HC 10 9 8 7 6 5 4 3 2
PB 10 9 8 7 6 5 4 3 2 1

ABOUT THE AUTHOR

Connie Colwell Miller is a writer, editor, and instructor who lives in Mankato, Minnesota, with her four children. She has written over 80 books for young children. She likes to tell stories to her kids to teach them important life lessons.

ABOUT THE ILLUSTRATOR

Victoria Assanelli was born during the autumn of 1984 in Buenos Aires, Argentina. She spent most of her childhood playing with her grandparents, reading books, and drawing doodles. She began working as an illustrator in 2007, and has illustrated several textbooks and storybooks since.